# Those Magical
# Manatees

# Those Magical Manatees

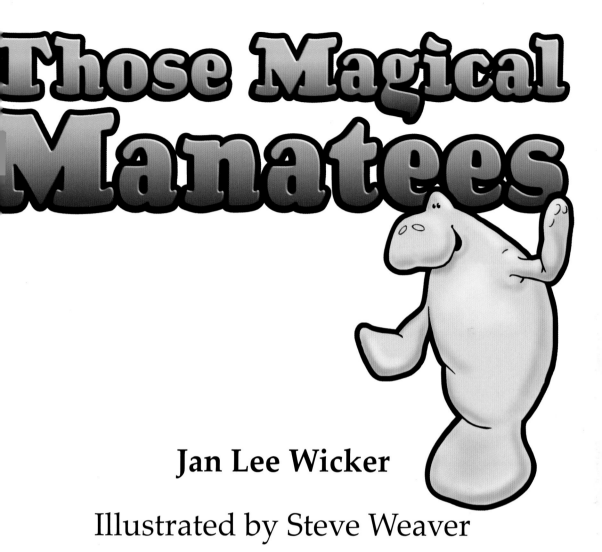

Jan Lee Wicker

Illustrated by Steve Weaver

Pineapple Press, Inc.
Sarasota, Florida

Photographs © 2008:
Cathy A. Beck, USGS, pages 10, 16, 22, 26, 38, 44; Marc Ellis, pages 32, 36; William Garvin, Compliments of Homosassa Springs Wildlife State Park, pages 8, 34, 42; Gail Mitchell, Compliments of Homosassa Springs Wildlife State Park, page 18; Laura M. Osteen, pages 20, 24, 28, 30, 40; Doug Stamm, www.stammphoto.com, page 2; Susan Strawbridge, Compliments of Homosassa Springs Wildlife State Park, page 46

Inquiries should be addressed to:

Pineapple Press, Inc.
P.O. Box 3889
Sarasota, Florida 34230

www.pineapplepress.com

Library of Congress Cataloging-in-Publication Data

Wicker, Jan Lee, 1953-
Those magical manatees / Jan Lee Wicker. -- 1st ed.
p. cm.
Includes index.
ISBN 978-1-56164-382-0 (hardback : alk. paper) -- ISBN 978-1-56164-383-7 (pbk. : alk. paper)
1. Manatees--Juvenile literature. I. Title.
QL737.S63W53 2008
599.55--dc22
2007040415

First Edition
10 9 8 7 6 5 4 3 2 1

Design by Steve Weaver
Printed in China

To my son Lee, whose love of nature is contagious

# Contents

# What is a Manatee?

A manatee is a slow-moving animal that lives in the water. It is gray and very big. Its tail looks like a beaver's tail and moves up and down for swimming. A manatee's skin is thick and feels like sandpaper. It has two front flippers for steering. The manatee's eyes are small and look like buttons. Because of their size and their gentle nature, manatees are often called "gentle giants." They are also known as "sea cows."

# Why are manatees magical?

When sailors first saw manatees, they thought the manatees were beautiful mermaids. The sailors heard the squeaking sounds that manatees make and dreamed that the "mermaids" were singing to them. They must have been out to sea way too long! Christopher Columbus wrote that the mermaids were not as beautiful as the sailors had said. He didn't think the bald-headed manatees with wrinkled skin and no front teeth were very pretty.

West African Manatee

Amazonian Manatee

West Indian Manatee

# How many different kinds of manatees are there?

There are 3 different kinds of manatees. The West Indian manatee is found in Florida. It lives in salt, fresh, or brackish water. Brackish water is a mix of ocean water and fresh water. It is not as salty as ocean water. The Amazonian manatee has smooth skin and it doesn't have toenails on its flippers. It is smaller than the West Indian manatee. It lives in fresh water. Not much is known about the West African manatee, but it is the most endangered of the three. It is hunted for its meat, leather, and oil.

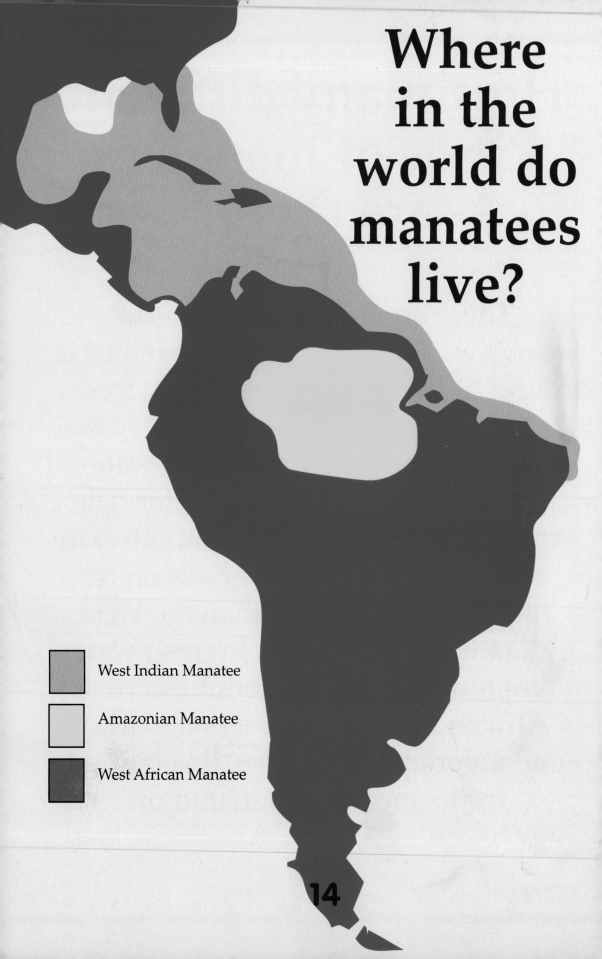

# Where in the world do manatees live?

West Indian Manatee

Amazonian Manatee

West African Manatee

14

The West Indian manatees live in
southeastern United States, the
Caribbean Islands, eastern Mexico, and
Central America. They can be found
along the northern and eastern coast of
South America from Venezuela to Brazil.
The Amazonian manatee is found along
the Amazon River in Brazil. The West
African manatee is found along the west
coast of Africa from Mauritania
to Angola.

# What do manatees eat?

Manatees don't eat meat. They eat plants that live in the water. They eat 100–150 pounds of plants a day. They spend up to 8 hours a day eating. Can you imagine eating vegetables all day long? Manatees use their lips and flippers to help them move the plants into their mouths.

SALAD BAR

# Is a manatee a mammal?

Yes. You may notice that they don't have fur like most mammals. Their bodies are dotted with short hairs or whiskers, like an elephant. They breathe air. They don't lay eggs, but have live babies. Manatees nurse (give milk to) their babies. Manatees are warm-blooded like we are. Their body temperature stays the same. It doesn't change with the outside temperature.

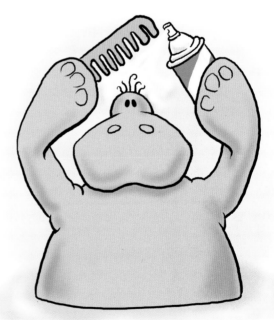

# Do manatees have teeth?

Yes. Manatees don't have front teeth, but have big back teeth called molars. They have 24–32 molars. These grind their food. The sand that is on the grass they eat wears out their teeth. When their teeth get worn out, they fall out. New ones push forward. That is why their teeth are called "marching molars." They even use rope they find near boat docks to floss their teeth, just as you use dental floss to floss your teeth.

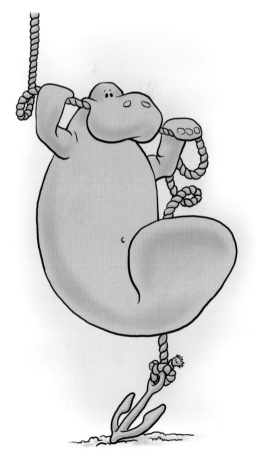

# Why do manatees swim upside down?

Do you have a favorite swim stroke? Sometimes it's fun to swim on your back. Maybe it's the same for manatees. Sometimes they do barrel rolls, too. They probably swim upside down to relax and rest. Sometimes they rest on the bottom, lying on their backs.

# How big are manatees?

A grown-up manatee is about 10 feet long. That is as tall as a basketball hoop. They weigh around 1,500 pounds. That's more than a cow weighs. Some manatees weigh 3,000 pounds. Manatees can live to be about 60 years old, but usually don't. The reason is that contact with humans and their motor boats can hurt or kill manatees.

# How many babies do manatees have?

Manatees have one baby at a time. It takes more than a year for a calf (baby manatee) to be born. It is born head-first or tail-first. The calf weighs about 60 pounds. It is 4 feet long. It nurses for 1–2 years. The nursing glands are under the mother's flippers. A manatee doesn't have babies until she is 4–5 years old.

# Why aren't there many manatees?

Manatees only have one baby every 2–5 years. Manatees have no natural enemies, but people are a big problem for them. Water pollution, getting caught in fishing lines, eating trash, and getting hurt by boats are some ways manatees are killed. In the United States manatees are protected by state and federal laws. These laws set speed limits for boats and protect the manatees' habitats. Yet there are only about 3,000 West Indian manatees left in Florida.

# How can you tell manatees apart?

Scientists use the scars manatees get from being hit by boats to tell adult manatees apart. Most adults have been hit at least once by a boat or its propeller. Some manatees have lost their flippers because they got twisted up in fishing lines.

# Can manatees see well?

Yes. They are far-sighted. This means they can see things that are far away better than things that are close. People who are far-sighted need glasses to read. Manatees don't have eyelashes to protect their eyes. They have an extra eyelid that is clear and opens from the side. Manatees don't have many neck bones. This means they can't turn their heads like we can, so they have to turn their whole bodies to look at something.

# How do manatees communicate?

Manatees make squeaks, chirps, whistles, and grunts. When manatees are upset the squeak changes to a shorter sound. If scared, they make longer squeaks that sound like screams. When a calf wants to nurse, it will cry until its mother nurses it. Manatees touch each other as another way of communication too. They may chase each other, do somersaults, play with rope, or even body surf together. They have been seen even kissing each other!

manatee ear bone

# Can manatees hear well?

Yes. Manatees don't have ears on the outside of their heads like we do. They have two tiny ear holes just behind the eyes. Their ear bones are very big. Scientists can tell the age of a manatee by counting the growth rings inside their ear bones—one ring for every year.

# Why is it bad to give manatees water or food?

Manatees will come back to where they can get free food and water. They like drinking water out of a water hose and eating heads of lettuce. When manatees are eating they do not pay attention to what is around them. They could even stay in boating areas to get free food. That is how they get hit by boats. This would be just as dangerous as children playing in traffic in the middle of the street.

PLEASE DO NOT FEED MANATEES

# What is the green stuff on the backs of manatees?

It is algae. Algae are plants that grow in the water. You can see algae growing in a dirty aquarium. It looks green or brown. Algae need water and light to grow. The algae may help protect manatees against the sun. How would you like algae rubbed on your back instead of sunscreen?

# How do manatees sleep?

They can sleep on the bottom or top of the water. Manatees can also sleep upside down, on their heads, or on their sides. They take short naps day and night. They spend 2–12 hours a day resting. They breathe every 3–5 minutes. Manatees can hold their breath up to 20 minutes.

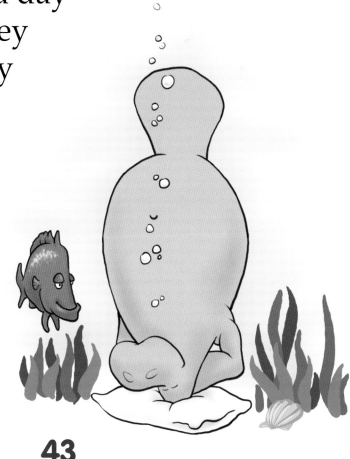

# Do manatees migrate?

Yes. They migrate in the winter to find warmer water. They need to live in water that is 70 degrees. Although manatees look fat, they do not have much blubber (or body fat) to keep them warm. Manatees are the slowest-moving aquatic mammals. They usually swim about 3–5 miles per hour. This is the same speed as the fastest human swimmer. Manatees can swim in short bursts of 15–20 miles per hour.

# What can you do to protect the manatees?

If you live anywhere near water where manatees live, be careful what you put on your yard or driveway. Pesticides, gasoline, and other chemicals end up in our rivers and oceans. You can help protect manatees even if you live in an area that is not close to the water. You can help by adopting a manatee. The "Save a Manatee" website will show you how. The money is used to learn more about manatees and to pay for scientists to rescue hurt manatees. It is also used to get more laws passed to protect manatees.

47

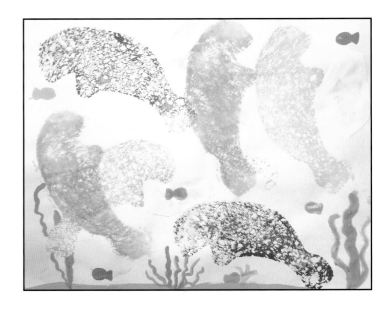

## Manatee Sponge Print

Materials needed:
| | |
|---|---|
| heavy paper | paint |
| thin sponge | flat pan |
| paper towel | white paper |
| tempera | |

Cut the shape of a manatee's body from heavy paper for your pattern. Using the pattern, cut a sponge manatee. (The thin, flat sponges at craft shops are easier to trace and cut.)
Wet the sponge and squeeze it out. You need to get most of the water out. Wrap a dry paper towel around the sponge and squeeze again. Pour a small amount of paint into the flat pan.
Lightly place the sponge into the paint. Press the sponge lightly onto the white paper. With sponge painting you want to see the texture of the sponge. Use different colors to make a colorful herd of manatees on your paper. You can paint in little fish and some sea plants with other colors if you like.

## Splatter Paint Manatee

Materials needed:

| | |
|---|---|
| 2 colors of tempera paint | manatee pattern |
| 2 old toothbrushes | tape |
| colored paper | container for paints |

Roll your tape and tape the back of the manatee pattern onto the middle of the colored paper. Dip the bristles of a toothbrush into some paint. Holding your toothbrush close to the paper, use your finger to quickly rub along the bristles many times. The paint should splatter all over your paper. Make sure to go around the edge of the pattern. When you have the desired amount of paint, spatter again with the other color. Let it dry overnight. Carefully remove the pattern. You can draw lines to show the mouth and flippers, and a dot for the eye.

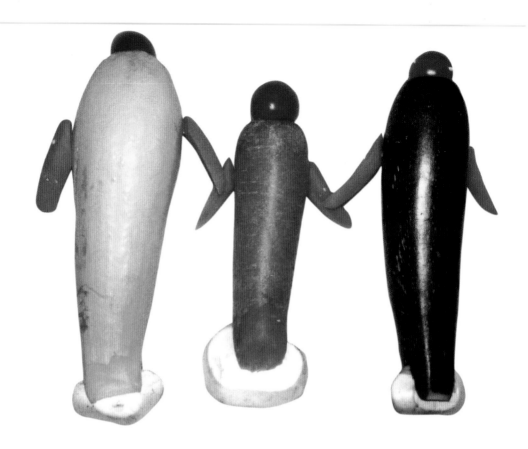

## Veggi-tee

Materials needed:

baby carrot, vertically sliced in half for the 2 flippers
large zucchini, squash, or carrot for the body
sliced mushroom for the tail

grape tomato for the head
4 or more toothpicks
knife (to be used by adult)
your favorite salad dressing

Using a knife, cut off the tip of the tomato and the bigger end of the vegetable you are using for the body. Stick the toothpick into the tomato and attach it to the body. Cut a wedge into the smaller end of the body and slide in the mushroom. Stick toothpicks into the bigger ends of the baby carrot slices. Attach the flippers onto the sides of the body. Dip parts of your veggi-tee into the salad dressing and eat it up. Yum!

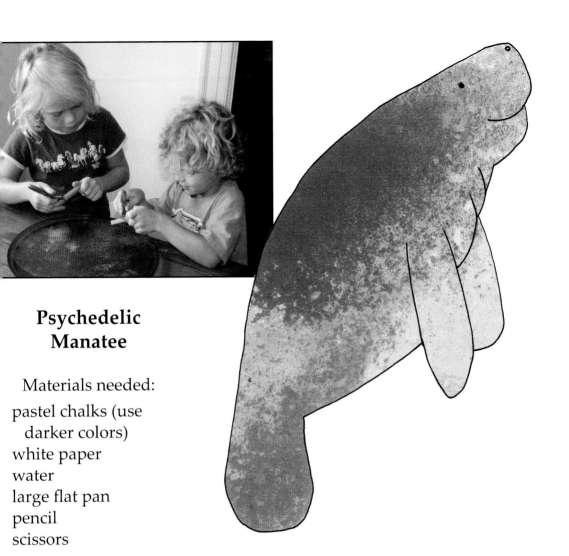

## Psychedelic Manatee

Materials needed:

pastel chalks (use
   darker colors)
white paper
water
large flat pan
pencil
scissors

Pour 1 inch of water into the pan so water is touching all sides. Open the scissors and use them to scrape the sides of the chalk so it falls on top of the water. (Don't touch the water or the chalk flakes will sink.) Try to use at least 3–4 colors. Once the top of the water is covered with chalk flakes, take the paper and lay it on top of the water briefly so the water sticks the chalk to the paper. (It might be a good idea for an adult to do this part.) Pull the paper out and lay it flat. Once it is dry, using the pattern here, carefully trace a manatee onto the paper. Cut it out and add the lines to make the flippers and face.

# Glossary

**algae** – (al-jee) simple plants that grow in the water

**blubber** – the fat found in sea animals

**calf** – a baby cow or bull (manatee females are cows, the males are bulls)

**far-sighted** – able to see things far away easier than to see things close up

**habitat** – the place where a plant or animal lives

**mammal** – an animal that can produce milk for its young

**mermaids** – a creature with the head and upper body of a woman and the tail of a fish (they are not real)

**migrate** – to move from one place to another when the seasons change

**molar** – back tooth used for grinding up food

**pesticide** – a chemical used to kill insects

**propeller** – the blades attached to the motor that turn to make the boat move

# Where to Learn More about Manatees

## Books

Feeney, Kathy. Our Wild World Series—*Manatees*. Minnetonka, MN: Northwood Press, 2001.

Haley, Jan. J. *Rooker, Manatee*. Bemidji, MN: Focus Publishing, Inc., 2002.

Kalman, Bobbie. *Endangered Manatees*. New York: Crabtree Publishing Co., 2006.

Maden, Mary. *The Great Manatee Rescue*. Kill Devil Hills, NC: Dog and Pony Publishing, 2002.

Tate, Susan. *Mary Manatee*. St. Petersburg, FL: Nags Head Art, Inc., 2005.

## Websites

www.manateewoman.com

www.savethemanatee.org

www.nationalgeographic.com/kids

http://cars.er.usgs.gov/Manatees/manatees.html

# About the Author

Jan Lee Wicker has taught children in pre-kindergarten through first grade for the last 25 years. She saw her first manatee at Homosassa Springs in Florida. She wears her manatee hat when she teaches her kindergarten students about manatees. She and her husband Chris live in Roanoke Rapids, North Carolina. They have two grown sons, Paul and Lee.

You can visit Mrs. Wicker's website at www.pinkflamingolady.com.

# Index

(Numbers in **bold** refer to photographs.)

Here are some other books from Pineapple Press on related topics. For a complete catalog, write to Pineapple Press, P.O. Box 3889, Sarasota, Florida 34230-3889, or call (800) 746-3275. Or visit our website at www.pineapplepress.com.

*Those Amazing Alligators* by Kathy Feeney. Illustrated by Steve Weaver, photographs by David M. Dennis. Alligators are amazing animals, as you'll see in this book. Discover the differences between alligators and crocodiles; learn what alligators eat, how they communicate, and much more. Ages 5–9.

*Those Beautiful Butterflies* by Sarah Cussen. Illustrated by Steve Weaver. This book answers 20 questions about butterflies—their behavior, why the look the way they do, how they communicate, and much more. Ages 5–9.

*Those Delightful Dolphins* by Jan Lee Wicker. Illustrations by Steve Weaver. Learn the difference between a dolphin and a porpoise, find out how dolphins breathe and what they eat, and learn how smart they are and what they can do. Ages 5–9.

*Those Excellent Eagles* by Jan Lee Wicker. Illustrated by Steve Weaver, photographs by H. G. Moore III. Learn all about those excellent eagles— what they eat, how fast they fly, why the American bald eagle is our country's national bird. You'll even make some edible eagles. Ages 5–9.

*Those Funny Flamingos* by Jan Lee Wicker. Illustrated by Steve Weaver. Flamingos are indeed funny birds. Learn why those funny flamingos are pink, stand on one leg, eat upside down, and much more. Ages 5–9.

*Those Outrageous Owls* by Laura Wyatt. Illustrated by Steve Weaver, photographs by H. G. Moore III. Learn what owls eat, how they hunt, and why they look the way they do. You'll find out what an owlet looks like, why horned owls have horns, and much more. Ages 5–9.

*Those Peculiar Pelicans* by Sarah Cussen. Illustrated by Steve Weaver, photographs by Roger Hammond. Find out how much food those peculiar pelicans can fit in their beaks, how they stay cool, and whether they really steal fish from fishermen. And learn how to fold up an origami pelican. Ages 5–9.

*Those Terrific Turtles* by Sarah Cussen. Illustrated by Steve Weaver, photographs by David M. Dennis. You'll learn the difference between a turtle and a tortoise, and find out why they have shells. Meet baby turtles and some very, very old ones, and even explore a pond. Ages 5–9.